Notes on
DIRECTING

Romeo + Juliet
2004

Edward

Notes on

DIRECTING

FRANK
HAUSER

RUSSELL
REICH

Published by RCR Creative Press, New York, New York

Interior design by Pneuma Books, LLC.
visit www.pneumabooks.com for more information

Publisher's Cataloging-in-Publication
(*Provided by Quality Books, Inc.*)

Hauser, Frank, 1922-
    Notes on directing / by Frank Hauser and Russell
Reich. -- 1st ed.
    p. cm.
Includes bibliographical references and index.
    LCCN 2002094557
    ISBN 0-9724255-0-0

    1. Theater--Production and direction. 2. Acting
I. Reich, Russell. II. Title.

PN2053.H38 2003   792'.0233
                         QBI33-815

    10 09 08 07 06 05 04 03   5 4 3 2

RꞒR CREATIVE PRESS

NEW YORK

IN MEMORY OF
BILL STILES

Table of Contents

Table of Contents

Table of Contents

Table of Contents

Preface

Human beings have been performing at least since our cave-dwelling ancestors enacted the hunt before the rest of the tribe. And yet, those who have studied theatre or film—especially those with an interest in directing—know how rare it is to get solid, time-tested, and craftsman-like guidance on what to watch out for, when to intervene, and how to avoid common mistakes.

Throughout my own schooling and apprenticeship as a young director, I was hungry for such fundamental principles and solid advice. Aristotle and Stanislavski had done their part, but who, I wondered, were the current standard-bearers? Who, if anyone, could give reliable counsel on actors' tendencies and behaviors, common audience perceptions, or effective interventions to familiar rehearsal conundrums and performance crises? Who, in short, knew the rules?

Then I met Frank Hauser.

...

It was the late 1980s. I had just graduated from college, quit a job to which I was ill suited at a bank on Wall Street, and set off for London in search of a directing career.

There was Frank, one of my teachers, a scarecrow of a man with a scratchy voice, a quick wit, and a penchant for impish puns and gentle teasing. His rumpled garb and folksy manner belied his considerable achievements; during his nearly fifty-year career, he ran the professional theatre at Oxford University, directed numerous productions in London and New York, and taught and directed many who were or would later become royalty of the British stage, including Alec Guinness, Richard Burton, Judi Dench, and Ian McKellen.

Around the time I met him, Frank was at the coda of his career with three productions running simultaneously in the West End. After completing our class work in London, Frank invited me to

Chichester, a festival theatre town in southern England where I apprenticed as his assistant director on a production of *A Man for All Seasons* by Robert Bolt.

One day before beginning rehearsal, a surprise. Frank handed me a collection of twelve neatly typewritten pages, the first of which modestly stated his subject: *Notes on Directing*.

"You might find these helpful," he said.

The *Notes* were the great gift of his collected wisdom—gathered over his distinguished career and polished to a sharp edge. Distributed informally to friends and students, Frank's *Notes* told how he spoke to actors, how he analyzed a scene, how he kept rehearsals buoyant and efficient...in short, how he went about bringing a story to life.

Frank's directing technique in rehearsal wasn't nearly as doctrinaire as his *Notes* might have indicated, but they did capture his pith and efficiency; his quick, almost surgical intervention; his concentrated, deceptively simple guidance to actors that is, like him, sometimes easy to underestimate.

As a director, Frank elaborates when he must, but with seeming reluctance. He stops a bit short, expecting you as the actor or student to fill in the gaps and take some responsibility as an active participant in the conversation. In other words, you have a role to play. The assertions are his, the rumination and implementation, yours. Only after some time does one catch on to how much he is accomplishing by doing and saying seemingly little—a sure sign of a skilled director and teacher at work.

Fifteen years after we met, I approached Frank with the idea to expand his twelve pages into a book.

All of his original *Notes* are still here. But they are supplemented with other techniques and teachings I observed Frank demonstrate in rehearsal, as well as with additional material based on my own experience and the teachings of others.

We have given the book the voice of an assertive instructor, one whose favorite words are "do this," "don't do that," "always," and "never." Frank and I could have taken a milder, more suggestive approach, but better, we thought, to overshoot and provoke than to risk having all the impact of a marshmallow.

Certainly it's appropriate to question the dogmatic assertions found here — to struggle with them, debate them, hate them even. Our hope, though, is that the reader will have nearly an impossible time *ignoring* them.

RUSSELL REICH

Notes on
Notes on Directing

by Frank Hauser

You'll be told, "Directing can't be told. Each director must find his own way, build his own relationship with his fellow workers."

All very true. What follows is not a book of instructions—though to save time it sometimes sounds like one. Some of the notes are optional. Some (like 65. Never, NEVER bully and 41. Don't keep actors hanging about needlessly) are not. In general, it's an account of how I work, and as such it is meant to help the student director save time—his own and everyone else's.

But the most important things—the passion, the talent you bring to your work—these are for you alone.

FEBRUARY 1992

———⟨⟩———

More Notes on
Notes on Directing

by Russell Reich

In addition to being of interest to aspiring directors, this book is intended to serve as a helpful stimulant to experienced practitioners open to considering new perspectives or ways of working. And it is for film-makers, theatregoers, and enthusiasts who want to peer more closely into the hidden process of creating a shared, live experience.

The book is intended to be used not simply as a "how to," but as a tool. It can be read in at least three directions:

1. A linear approach from start to finish tracks roughly with the course of the rehearsal process, addressing a director's concerns in the general order they are likely to arise.

2. A random, pointillist approach is also appropriate. For instance, while on the way to rehearsal or waiting for the actors to show up, one can open the book to wherever whimsy dictates and get a taste of what might just be needed for that day's proceedings.

3. A crisscross line of attack emerges by following the occasional cross-references from note to note. These connections reveal conceptual relationships and highlight larger themes that may not be readily apparent across relatively broad expanses of the material.

In addition, the table of contents and index provide ready references whenever guidance is needed on a particular topic.

Beware: Actors aren't machines, scripts aren't technical drawings, and this book is no substitute for thinking and responding with fluidity in the moment. When humming properly, rehearsals and performances are ever-changing, real-life experiences. Rule-of-thumb prescriptions, therefore, cannot be applied indiscriminately.

Accordingly, the reader will likely find contradictions within these pages (compare, for example, the dual directives in appendix III to keep things simple *and* add variety). No doubt this will frustrate purists, but just as any director must choose his or her tools and tactics every moment of each rehearsal, the reader will have to discern when to apply a particular truth and when to be alert to its exceptions and contradictions.

This book alone will not make anyone a good artist, a good craftsman, or a true professional. Some things must still be learned and understood not through words, but through experience. The work with others, the inevitable failures, the rich discoveries and unanticipated rewards that arise from persistence, experimentation, commitment, and enthusiasm are still, as Frank hinted in his introduction, for you as a director to develop and earn on your own.

NOVEMBER 2002

It is necessary to learn from others' mistakes.
You will not live long enough to make them
all yourself.

ADMIRAL HYMAN G. RICKOVER
(1900—1986)

I

Understanding the Script

1. **Read the play.**
   Or hear the play from its source by having the playwright read it to you.

   Unplug the telephone, don't answer the door, just sit and read it through. At the end make notes or comments, very simple ones... "Opening a bit boring." "Don't get the bit about the will." "Last bit very moving."

2. **Take a break and read it again.**
   This time let yourself wander: Think about the look of it, the sort of actors you're going to need, whether the problems you saw the first time round are solving themselves.

3. **If you have any choice, try to fit the designers to the work.**

   A production of Chekhov's *Three Sisters* designed by Francis Bacon might be fun, but it probably wouldn't help the cast or the audience any.

4. **Don't finalize the designs too early.**

   You'll always be pressured by the workshops, but hold them off as long as possible. Your ideas will certainly change as you get to know the play better.

5. **Read each character's part through as if you were playing it.**

   Skip the scenes you are not in and concentrate on your own lines. This often gives you a more vivid idea of the character and helps in casting.

6. **Don't overstudy.**

   "I know every word of this text by heart" is a favorite director's boast, but it can restrict your imagination. It's the actor's job to remember his lines, not yours. Sometimes just guessing how a scene goes can make you think more freely.

7. **Learn to love a play you don't particularly like.**

   You may be asked—or may choose—to direct a play that, for any number of reasons, you don't think is very good. In such cases it is better to focus and build on the play's virtues than attempt to repair its inherent problems.

8. **Identify the story's compelling question.**

   Every good play has a basic "will she or won't she…," an essential question about the central character(s) that keeps the audience interested, a question around which all the action revolves. Think of Shakespeare's *Hamlet*: Will the prince avenge his father's murder? Ibsen's *A Doll's House*: Will Nora keep her secret from Torvald?

   As the director, you must understand what primarily keeps the audience interested in the ongoing action.

9. **Realize that the human experience is one of suffering and the resolution of suffering.**

   Legitimate questions to ask of any script: How are these characters suffering? What are they doing to resolve their suffering?

10. **Appreciate that character is the result of conduct.**
    As Aristotle taught us, we know people primarily by what they *do*. What others say about them, or what they say about themselves, may or may not be true.

11. **Understand that plays depict people in extraordinary circumstances.**
    It's not everyday life on stage, but something more: something extreme, defining, life-changing.

    What is the source of these special circumstances? Arthur Miller said, "The structure of the play is always the story of how the birds came home to roost."

    That is, the consequences of something someone once did always come back to haunt the characters in the *now* of the play. These acts from the past permeate the story; they threaten the ordinary circumstances and values of the characters' lives, and they force choices to be made.

    As Edward Albee said, "That's what happens in plays, yes? The shit hits the fan."

12. **Recognize that the struggle is more important than the outcome.**
    Whether the characters accomplish what they set out to accomplish is not critical. What *is* important is that

their intentions are clear—that they go about their struggles, encounter obstacles, and make moment-to-moment choices about what they need to do to achieve their goals. Their choices in the face of clear and compelling circumstances are what make them interesting; characters either change their circumstances or are changed by them.

The audience witnesses each character's journey and vicariously goes along with them: "I agree with that." "What did he do that for?" "Now *that* was an interesting thing to do; I never would have thought of such a clever tactic."

Towards the end of the play, as the audience anticipates an impending collision or miracle coming, they won't care about *what* happens nearly as much as they'll care about how the characters *react* to what happens. Again, the emotional journey is more important than the destination.

13. **Realize that the end is in the beginning.**
    In all the best material, the outcome is inevitable and inherent in the opening moment and in every moment in between. From the audience's perspective, this can only be understood and appreciated *backwards*, after the play has run its course. The audience,

if they choose, will see every element was essential; every moment from the first to the last contributed to the final resolution or explosion.

This is really about you, as the director, aiming for *elegance*—the absence of anything superfluous. (See 96. Every object tells.)

This fully cohesive quality is easy to describe but hard to create. Nevertheless, it is critical for the director to identify the unifying structure of the play to which every subordinate element contributes.

14. **Express the core of the play in as few words as possible.**

Not more than a dozen words should do it. This is what the whole shooting match is aiming at, so:

    A. What is the first impression the actors and the design should make on the audience?

    B. What should their final impression be as the play ends?

    C. How do you propose getting from A to B?

II

The Director's Role

15. **You are the obstetrician.**

    You are not the parent of this child we call the play. You are present at its birth for *clinical* reasons, like a doctor or a midwife. Your job most of the time is simply to do no harm.

    When something does go wrong, however, your awareness that something is awry—and your clinical intervention to correct it—can determine whether the child will thrive or suffer, live or die.

16. **Just tell the story...**

    ...as believably, as excitingly as possible. Whatever does not tell the story should be subject to a very fishy examination.

    It does sometimes happen that decoration will salvage a weak play, but we are concerned with strong plays, and the audience has come to the theatre to *be-*

lieve, to respond to the magical words, "Once upon a time...," not to admire a laser show.

17. **Don't always connect all the dots.**
    Give the audience a role in filling in what's happening. That is, give them all the dots they need but don't connect all the dots for them.

    For example, Julie Taymor's designs for the musical *The Lion King* offered the audience the choice to look at each actor's face or at the face of the puppet character each actor was operating. This allowed the audience to imaginatively invent the illusion moment by moment along with the performers and was far more artful than putting humans in animal suits. *That* would have been a clear example of connecting too many dots.

18. **Keep the audience guessing.**
    But make sure the spectators are aware of those little hints that will become important later: Romeo's potential for violence, Saint Joan's tidal wave way with opposition.

    Play against the obvious, but don't cheat. That is, don't rig the evidence so that when the climax comes, the audience feels, "Well, I didn't expect that, and, what's more, the way they told the story, I don't believe it."

19. **Don't try to please everybody.**
   Bill Cosby said, "I don't know the formula for success, but I do know the formula for failure: trying to please everybody."

   With both the authority and the responsibility to stage the play well, you will inevitably have to make some unpopular decisions. Accept the grumbling. Be strong and calm in the face of opposition—and realize that normal conversation includes a good portion of complaint.

20. **You can't have everything.**
   Harold Clurman said that if you get 60 percent of what you saw in your head onto the stage, you're doing very well.

   There may be no way to close this deficit, but do expect it. Not everything is within your control.

21. **Don't expect to have all the answers.**
   You're the leader, but you're not alone. The other artists are there to contribute as well. Use them.

Elia Kazan's concise directing advice was: "Before you do anything, see what talent does."

22. **No actor likes a lazy director, or an ignorant one.**
You should certainly know the meaning (and the pronunciation) of every word, every reference, every foreign phrase.

23. **Assume that everyone is in a permanent state of catatonic terror.**
This will help you approach the impossible state of infinite patience and benevolence that actors and others expect from you.

24. **Lighten up.**
Nobody dies if things go wrong; millions of dollars are not lost (you should be so lucky to have the chance). Children do not starve as a result of a bad rehearsal, performance, or review. Be passionate, sure, but know when not to take yourself too seriously.

When you need a favor or have a request that is perhaps beyond someone's ordinary responsibilities or inclinations, you can cool your ardor and enormously increase your effectiveness by adding, "I'll understand completely if it's not something you're able to do right now."

25. Don't change the author's words.
Director Lloyd Richards said that if you continually find yourself itching to make changes to a script, consider whether you should give up directing and take up playwriting.

26. You perform most of the day.
A general, very important note.

As a director, you are there to explain things to people and to tell them what to do (even if that means telling them to do whatever they want). Speak clearly. Speak briefly. Guard against the director's first great vice—rabbiting on, making the same point again and again, getting laughs from your inimitable (and interminable) anecdotes, wasting time.

And guard against the second great vice, the idiot fill-in phrases: "You know," "I mean," "Sort of...," "Kind of...," "Er, er, um...." These are bad enough in ordinary conversation; coming from someone who may be giving instructions for up to three hours a day, they can be a justification for homicide.

27. **It is not about you.**

    Yes, there is a component of ego reward involved in directing, but it is a built-in perk; no need to seek it out. Instead, serve the play by serving others, particularly the playwright, the actors, and the audience. Ask yourself: What do I have to *give* to this play? What *right* do I have to take this audience's time and money? What am I giving to this audience that makes their investment in this work worthwhile *to them*?

28. **The best compliment for a director: "You seemed from the beginning to know exactly what you wanted."**

    Actors and others will follow you even if they disagree with your direction. But they will not follow if you are afraid to lead. A clear, confident presence and strong direction are highly reassuring to everyone.

III

Casting

29. Directing is mostly casting.

Some say directing is 60 percent casting, others say 90 percent. Regardless, it's a lot. There is not a more important single decision you will make during the production than who you put into a role. (Though your choice of designers—set, costume, lights, and sound—is right up there and is, of course, also a kind of casting.)

Director Ron Eyre once said that when you place someone in a role, you are plugging in to his or her entire "life stream." As in a marriage, you are taking responsibility for living with that person's unique constellation of virtues and vices. Certain doors will be open, others will be tightly closed, and still other doors may open with a slight nudge.

Learn as much as you can about what you're getting yourself into. In addition to an audition, inquire of others about the person. Is she polite, professional, and re-sponsive? Speak with her. Study the résumé carefully: Has this person done roles like this before? This size? This style? This level? Take the time to find the answers. Yes, you might still get fooled from time to time, but that's hardly a reason to neglect your due diligence.

30. **Don't expect the character to walk in the door.**
If he does, hesitate before casting him. It is all-too-common to see the perfect audition lead to a per-formance that's lacking.

Why is this? A walking, talking character is quite different from a trained, professional actor. A true professional will grow into a role, analyze the script and develop insights, anticipate and deal with prob-lems, create the required illusion, and develop a rela-tionship with the other characters and the audience that no amount of "typing" can easily achieve. In short, a pro will know what to do. And it frees you from the onerous task of nursing one actor's per-formance at the cost of neglect to the others. That would be sure to sow resentment.

An important distinction, then, to make at this early stage in the process is not, "Is he convincing as the character?" but "Can he play it?"

This is not to say you should ignore externals. Everything *tells* to an audience and nothing about the actor should undermine what the script calls for—a tall character should be played by a tall actor, a young ingénue by a young actress. But when forced to choose between two competing candidates, value skill and experience over the look or essence of an actor. Respect the mastery of craft that a skilled professional can provide.

31. **Put actors at ease, but don't befriend them.**
    When auditioning, actors know they are being looked at, listened to, evaluated, and judged. Their livelihood and self-image may hang in the balance. Everything you do or say as the auditor can have enormous emotional impact, so put actors at ease by letting them know *you* know what you're doing.

    Be informal and polite. Be conversational. Be *efficient.* (See 26. You perform most of the day, and 70. Please, PLEASE be decisive.)

    You cannot expect the actor's best work in an audition situation; it's too early in the process and too stressful. To maximize the actor's comfort and ensure the best possible work, be encouraging but keep complimentary remarks general—"That was fine." "Nice reading."—lest the actor misinterpret your praise as an indication of promised employment. Never be rude. Never make any promises. Don't make final decisions while the actor is in the room; no matter how stellar his audition, the next actor is sure to reveal possibilities you never imagined.

Do thank the actors. And let them know how and when they'll be contacted if there is interest.

32. Don't act with auditioners.

Your job in auditions is to observe and evaluate. Have the actor read with or to someone or something other than you: the wall, the chair, the production assistant, or the reader you brought in precisely for this purpose.

IV

First Read–Through

33. **Don't start with a great long brilliant speech.**
The actors will enjoy it—they'll laugh or frown with concentration, but they'll be far too nervous to take it in. Start with practicalities: rehearsal schedule, performance times. You need to say something about how you see the play, but showing the cast the designs will explain your general idea much more effectively.

34. **Don't let the actors mumble through the reading.**
Everyone hates first readings, but they often throw up insights that no one had imagined from solitary study.
    Go for intensity. Persuade the opening actors to commit themselves, to give it a full go, even if it means stopping and starting again. Reassure them that the others aren't snickering if they overshoot. They're thinking: how brave, damn good for her for giving it a try!

35. Talk it out after the reading.

You can launch your ideas at them while the play is still fresh in their minds and they are no longer scared of the ordeal. Get as many actors as possible to talk about it, but beware the know-all who has evolved obscure and elaborate theories about the Inner Meaning, spreading confusion and dismay.

36. Ask basic questions.

Good questions to ask early on: Where are they? Who is related to whom? How do people feel about each other? What time of year is it? Of day? How old are they? What dialect or accent might they have? Why does he enter the room? Why does she depart? Who's chasing whom?

Begin making distinctions: Is that action big or little? Is that intention nice or nasty? Big nice or little nice? Big nasty or little nasty? (See 55. Ask: Is it nice or nasty? Big or little?)

Also, analyze the playwright's intention notes (*e.g.* "he relaxes," or, an old favourite, "joking but not joking").

37. Mark the waves in a scene.

Where is formality broken by casualness? Romance by disappointment? When does the hunter take a new tack? When does the hunted apply new resistance? (See 53. Every scene is a chase scene.)

Discuss and delineate these internal scenes within scenes—not "French Scenes," which are defined by any entrance or exit of a character, but the individual, dramatic units where a few lines of dialogue or action have their own beginning, middle, and end.

V

Rehearsal Rules

38. Work from your strength.
Obviously, find out how you work best and do that: paraphrasing, playing animals, improv (short for "improvement," not "improvidence").

39. Rehearsals need discipline.
It's not your job to be everyone's friend all the time. Jump on lateness (an actor must phone through if humanly possible when he is going to be late), chattering noticeably as others are working, reading newspapers where the rehearsing actors can see...

40. Plan the schedule a week at a time.
Remember that in the early days, when you are all getting to know each other and the play, everything takes at least twice as long as you think it will.

41. Don't keep actors hanging about needlessly.

It demoralizes the entire cast. By all means get them there early so that you don't risk losing the impetus of the rehearsal, and if they have to wait for half an hour, that's life. But if you are really behind, offer them the chance to go away and come back later. And apologize.

42. Don't apologize when you don't have to.

Humorous self-deprecation can be very weakening within a company. Once again: *Don't try to be everyone's friend all the time.*

43. Make sure stage management get proper breaks.

It's all right for you to charge forward; you're the captain, but the troops get tired quicker. They don't have the same ego rewards you do to keep themselves as alert and motivated.

44. Say thank you.

Theatre manners dictate that cast and crew clearly and politely acknowledge an instruction or request from stage management. Enforce this sensible standard in your production.

Never allow any member of the company to be grand or rude to the stage managers. That sort of behaviour should have been stamped on but wasn't at drama school.

45. Include the crew.
The staff and crew are part of the creative process, not divorced from it. They can offer wonderful ideas, but are often too scared to say what they think. Solicit their opinion on the material with which they are involved and knowledgeable. (See 21. Don't expect to have all the answers.)

Set rules early for how people should offer creative contributions: privately, directly to you.

46. Always read the scene by yourself just before rehearsing it with the cast.
You will learn something every time you look at it.

47. Don't bury your head in the script.
Watch as much as possible. When you're running an act, and even more the whole play, don't sit taking notes all the time. A good method is to watch the first half without taking any notes at all. During the break, go through the text; you'll find that you can

recall how and what they all did and make your notes then. Ditto for part two.

When you are doing early runs, try watching one without making any notes at all. Just steep yourself in the play and the performance and watch as far as possible like a member of the audience. Let your notes be broader for that session.

There's one important exception here. During a single run-through late in the rehearsal process, don't watch the play at all. Just *listen*.

48. **Treat difficult moments as discoveries.**
When you encounter an obstacle in rehearsal it is often helpful just to leave it alone. For many problems, solutions are best uncovered in a separate, later step. Many other difficulties, left unmolested, simply solve themselves.

49. **Don't work on new material when people are tired.**
Review what you have already done.

50. **End rehearsals on an upbeat note.**
Consider thanking each person individually for his or her commitment and contribution.

51. Don't be grim.
Rehearsals should be sweaty, tough, and…enjoyable.
So should you.

52. If you choose to allow outsiders to see a late rehearsal…
…ask them specifics afterwards:

    A. What weren't you able to hear?

    B. What weren't you able to understand?

    C. What didn't hold your interest?

    D. How did you feel about it twenty-four hours later?

VI

Building Blocks

53. Every scene is a chase scene.

Character A wants something from Character B who doesn't want to give it. If he did, the scene would be over. Why does A want it? In order to...*what*? Why does B refuse?

Usually, when someone chases someone else they move toward their object, and the object, feeling the pressure, moves away. *Blocking*, that obscure mystery, is simply that. Lenin said, "Who? Whom?" That is, who is doing what to whom, and with what further aim? When the Ghost is hectoring Hamlet it is easy to see who is chasing whom, but look at the opening of *The Cherry Orchard* or *King Lear* and the answer is more problematic. Nevertheless, the chase underpins all dramatic structure. When you have learnt to see it, blocking becomes much more obvious and (still more important) a false move more glaringly apparent.

54. **The strength of the characters' wants equals the strength of the play.**

   If A just "kind of" wants twenty dollars from B, the action will be tepid. If B would just "kind of rather" doesn't want to give it, torpor sets in. If A is supposed to be strong, we can only realize his strength by the strength that B shows in opposition. By overcoming a powerful resistance, we measure A's toughness.

   Pounding your chest and flexing your muscles and then picking up a pillow impresses nobody.

   So if A delivers a long speech and B stands there nodding, knitting his brow, and being a good listener, the scene is on the floor. B must want to *abolish* A's speech almost as soon as it starts. He disagrees, he agrees but wants to put it another way, he feels A is trying to railroad him...there are dozens of reasons for him to want to interrupt. And in rehearsal it is a good idea to let B do just that, interrupt, so that A has to keep topping him. If there is no competition, the audience gets bored, because they can't see why A bothers to go on talking when his opponent has apparently conceded the game. (And incidentally, watch for the actor who signals, "This Is a Long Speech" by doubling his speed at the beginning.)

You are only as strong as the resistance you over-come.

55. Ask: Is it nice or nasty? Big or little?

If my line is "What a pretty sister you have," do you, as an actor, take that as nice or nasty? If it's nice, you tend to move toward me, however slightly. If it's nasty, you move away. If you don't move at all, you're dead.

How nice? How nasty? Big or little? The sum of all your reactions is your *character*. Discussions about this elusive critter we call character are, of course, neces-sary—particularly regarding practical matters. It is essential that all the actors agree on ages, relation-ships, and material situations, not to mention the plot of the play. (It is literally incredible how perfect-ly intelligent actors can be wildly awry in their grasp of the plot, mistaking mothers for sisters, getting the date of action a century out, and so on.)

56. Every actor has a tell.

A *tell* is what an actor does when he doesn't know what to do. It is a habitual behaviour that is complete-ly irrelevant to the task at hand and reveals itself at times of insecurity, fear, or lack of focus or imagina-tion. Look for stock postures, reliance on melodious

or heightened vocal inflections, repetitious move-
ments, or clichéd gestures. If it strikes you as false,
you're probably witnessing a tell.

Other common tells include knee slapping, "tsk"
sounds repeatedly inserted just before an actual line,
rising up on one's toes and dropping down again
(ridiculously common among Americans playing
British), and unnecessary facial scratching (absolutely epidemic).

One of the weakest and most common tells is a
pleading gesture of open hands facing upward and
outward toward the other actor(s). It's almost always
an indication of misplaced focus on the actor's own
emotions rather than on accomplishing a worthy objective. (David Mamet has taught that pleading is
highly undignified, akin to asking, "Can't you just
give me what I want?" rather than doing what's necessary to get it or earn it. See 67. Never express actions
in terms of feelings.)

While it may not be possible to know everything
about the actors with whom you are working, discovering their individual behavioural hints can be a valuable diagnostic indicator of when your intervention is
needed to clarify the character's situation. (See 66.
Keep actors on their task.)

VII

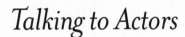

Talking to Actors

57. Discussion about character is best done piecemeal, as the work demands.

The great character analysis orgy usually takes place too early and too rigidly. The audience won't see your actor's dislike of his late grandmother, however useful that may be to him. What they will see is his line-by-line, scene-by-scene reaction to whatever is said and done—nice or nasty, big or little—while he is on the stage.

58. Start nice.

Cue the start of a scene with this: "Stand by. Lights coming up. Lights up."

It simulates the real thing, is far less scary than shouting, "Action!" and it creates a rehearsal ritual that puts everyone at ease.

59. Make a strong entrance.

Good motivational notes for entrances: "Today's the day! Tonight's the night! Enter to save the day!"

60. The actor's first job is to be heard.

If the first actors on stage can be heard clearly from the outset, the audience will feel comfortable enough to sit back and think: Ahhh! That's nice! I can hear! The audience will relax into a more receptive mood, the better to absorb all the other wonderfulness.

61. Sincerely praise actors early and often.

A very important note.

Rather than correcting your actors all the time, get into the habit of frequently telling them what they are doing *right*.

Also, be sure to tell your actors whenever they look good on stage. They'll trust you more knowing you are concerned with their appearance and dignity, and it will free them to go about their duties with less self-consciousness.

62. Talk to the character, not the actor.

When actors don't seem to have the right idea — close but no cigar — it is okay to say what they did was good because of the quality you were *looking for* but didn't get.

Example: A couple is saying goodbye to each other for the last time because the husband is on his way to the chopping block. They embrace, they cry, but something's missing. Say: "Wonderful! Touching! They're so *proud* of each other!"

Perhaps they weren't so proud, but they will get your point about what's really going on with the characters and their feelings as actors will go unwounded.

63. **Always sit and read a scene before blocking it.**
Even before you run any scene that was blocked the day before, sit round with the cast and read it again. Then your questions like, "Do you know what that word means?" or "Why does she say that now?" are easily asked and easily replied to. Once the actors are on their feet, the interruption can become confrontational: "He thinks I'm doing it badly!" "She's trying to catch me out!"

Ten minutes spent reading a scene or section before acting it can save hours later.

There's always time. Make time.

64. Do not expect too much too soon.

Many good actors just cannot implement the simplest actions or directions right away. There's nothing wrong with this. They may be thinking about or working on another element that's not apparent to you. Give them a day or two to assimilate what you tell them. (See 78. Always walk through changes.)

If they still don't respond, don't criticize. Gently remind them of what they did right in the past. This can work whether or not they actually did it right in the past; a reference to their fantastic work "last Tuesday" can provide just the right balance of positive reinforcement and corrective suggestion.

65. Never, NEVER bully…

…either by shouting or sarcasm or, worst of all, imitation. It will get a laugh and make an enemy. Using imitation to show an actor what he's doing wrong is allowable when all else has failed; but do it, if you have to do it at all, privately.

66. Keep actors on their task.

Just as a person who tries too hard to be funny won't be, an actor who tries too directly to hold an audience's attention is sure to bore them to tears.

The actor's job is not to hold the audience's attention. It is to do what needs to get done in the moment. *Your* job, then, is to keep actors focused on their objectives:

    A. "What do you want?"

    B. "What are you doing to get it?"

    C. "Is it working?"

    D. "Where's the resistance?"

67. **Never express actions in terms of feelings.**
Don't give actors undoable emotional directives such as: "Be disappointed." You are almost guaranteed an insincere result.

David Mamet has taught that an actor's feelings—like a surgeon's feelings, or a pilot's—are irrelevant to what needs to get done in the moment. His advice to actors: "Don't kill the patient because you don't *feel* like operating. Don't crash the plane because you don't *feel* like landing it." A true actor, like a true hero, does what is necessary regardless of his feelings.

An excellent way of expressing an action, however, is to prompt the actor to focus on how he wants the *other* person to feel.

Paul Newman once said the best direction he ever got was: "Crowd the guy."

68. **Tell actors: "Watch their eyes."**

To find out what someone is thinking (or feeling), actors should take a tip from boxers and watch their opponent's eyes.

You don't, however, act with your eyes (unless you're in front of a camera). You act primarily with your voice and body. Move toward the nice thing, away from the nasty thing.

69. **Actors are notoriously inaccurate about the quality of their own performances.**

When terrible, they think they're fine. When brilliant, they have no idea.

This is not as bad as it sounds. A lot of good acting has an essentially unselfconscious quality to it; actors *should* be unaware of themselves. (See 89. Actors must never aim for the laugh.) That's why they look to you to confirm they're all right.

Love them for this. Appreciate them for the extraordinary risks they are willing to take that the rest of us
fear too much even to contemplate.

70. **Please, PLEASE be decisive.**
As the director, you have three weapons: "Yes," "No,"
and "I don't know." Use them. *Don't dither*; you can
always change your mind later. Nobody minds that.
What they do mind is the two-minute agonizing
when all the actor has asked is, "Do I get up now?"
(Recall 26. You perform most of the day.)

71. **Being direct is appropriate for a director,
but not always.**
Some actors will clearly already know the answers to
the questions they ask you. In this case, they are really asking, "Am I okay?"
   In these situations, respond with additional questions of your own. Prompt them to understand and
accept their own sense of what is right. Hearing a director ask, "What do *you* think works here?" or "How
would *you* solve this?" is supportive, stimulating, and
flattering to any good actor. (Recall 21. Don't expect
to have all the answers.)

72. **Give actors corrective notes in private.**
    This will not only prevent damage caused by embar-
    rassing them in front of others, it will make them feel
    good to get individual attention. Let them feel as if
    they are sharing a secret with the director.

    If you can't give a critical note privately or skillful-
    ly, don't give it.

73. **Know your actors.**
    Some like a lot of attention; others want to be left
    alone. Some like written notes, some spoken. Get to
    know them. It doesn't have to take long. It's a good
    investment that will pay enormous benefits later.

74. **Don't give notes just prior to a performance or
    run-through.**
    Sure you want everything correctable to be correct-
    ed, but this just isn't the time.

    Safety issues are a glaring exception. You (or,
    preferably, stage management) must inform them,
    "There's a leaky pipe causing a small water puddle on
    the stage."

    The night before your big opening, it's okay to
    give general notes, but keep them few and positive.

75. **Don't assume people can take the harsh truth, even if they ask for it.**

   Temper bad news with three times as much good news (either order can work, but leave them off feeling good). When offering praise or criticism, be sincere and specific. (See 28. The best compliment for a director: "You seemed from the beginning to know exactly what you wanted.")

76. **Introduce bad news with "and" not "but."**

   DO: "The costume looks great, and when you keep your hat up, we can see your gorgeous face."

   DON'T: "The costume looks great, but you're not keeping your hat up, and we can't see your face."

77. **Include every single member of the cast in your note sessions.**

   Surely you know that in the theatre, silence is invariably taken for disapproval.

78. **Always walk through changes.**

It is not enough simply to discuss a new idea or change prior to performing it. Even the smallest business must be walked and spoken through *on stage* and *in character* prior to running it in front of an audience.

You cannot know all the possible consequences in advance. Good actors do an enormous amount of internal work based on the circumstances you and the script have set up. If you change those circumstances, you must give the actors the opportunity to adjust. (Recall 64. Do not expect too much too soon.)

When you make any change, be sure to include everyone who is in the scene. And don't forget to include the stage manager, who will likely be responsible for directing replacement actors and, in your absence, ensuring the show runs as you intend it to.

79. **Reverse the material.**

Stanislavsky says somewhere, "If you are playing a good man, look for the bad in him; if you are playing a bad man, look for the good in him." Obvious, but easy to forget.

An actor floating along on the surface of a character is cozy and boring.

80. **Don't play the end of scene at the beginning.**

Actors must delay as much as possible, delay that great twist, that surprise *denouement*. Remember what Bernard Shaw said about Elisabeth Bergner's Saint Joan: "She was half burnt when she first came on." And Bergner was a great actress.

81. **Play against the given condition.**

We all unknowingly reveal ourselves in our efforts to conceal or compensate for our secret, unspoken shortcomings.

For example, Jack Lemmon's advice on how to act drunk was, "Don't slur." This works because the action of speaking with (overly) clear diction betrays the character's effort to hide the undesirable and shameful state of drunkenness. That is, we convey a lack of physical control by concentrating instead on getting every physical action absolutely perfect.

Another example of this principle: For a good actor to play a bad actor, she should remember only the words and their proper order and nothing else. (See appendix 3: Simplicity.)

82. **Be gentle with actors just coming off book.**

It's a particularly vulnerable time, not a time to pursue new breakthroughs or to expect precision. If the cast stumbles, change blocking slightly, or discuss reactions and motives. This will free them up and stop them from being self-conscious.

83. **Frequently ask: "Who are you talking to?"**
Specific address by an actor increases audience interest, particularly when the target person changes while the character is speaking. As a rehearsal exercise, try addressing speeches or parts of speeches to an entirely new person from time to time. This can reveal new meaning.

84. **Anger is always preceded by pain.**
When an actor jumps to angry choices, look back together for the moment when the hurt occurs because that is what is more important—and more interesting.

85. **Tell actors: "Localize abstract things."**
That is, place mentioned items in space: "The church is *there*. Rome is *there*. I just spoke with the King, over in *that* direction."

86. **In later rehearsals, ask yourself: "Do I believe it?"**
    If the answer is no, chances are the actors are trying
    too hard to explain to the audience. It is the director's
    job to worry about whether the audience is getting it.
    The actors have a different task: truthfully going
    about achieving their goals on stage. And being heard.

87. **Consider late table work.**
    It is okay, after you have had a run-through or two, to
    sit people down again and analyze a scene line by line.
    This is appropriate late in rehearsals, when opening is
    drawing near and there is little sign of progress on an
    actor's part. In this situation, line readings somehow
    do not seem intrusive or inappropriate to most actors.
    They are often grateful for the guidance.

VIII

Getting a Laugh

88. Humor falls mostly into one of two categories.
British actor Edward Petherbridge aptly described the first category of humor when he said, "No one ever got a laugh out of something that wasn't someone else's tragedy."

But audiences also laugh at statements or actions they recognize as implicitly true. "When a thing is funny," wrote George Bernard Shaw, "search it for a hidden truth."

Part of your job as a director is to help the audience make connections that delight the mind. When an audience thinks, Ah! That suggests *this*, the accompanying reaction will often be simple laughter, a sure sign that you, the playwright, and the actors have done something right. (Recall 17. Don't always connect all the dots.)

89. **Actors must never aim for the laugh.**

Instead of going for what's funny, they must focus their attention on the situation. If they make it real and vital, the humor will be there too.

It is not their job to get a laugh; it is their job to go about achieving their objectives truthfully on stage. Help your actors identify what the character desperately wants. Help them understand the extreme and truthful circumstances the character is in. Audiences will be naturally delighted, drawn in, and amused by what's real and true.

Avoid telling actors what they did was funny or what they need to do to get a laugh. This is in consideration of their craft; by telling them the emotional result you want, you are revealing your lack of understanding of how they do what they do. (See 66. Keep actors on their task, and 67. Never express actions in terms of feelings.) Try to keep your interest in getting a laugh (or any other particular emotional result) to yourself.

90. **Play peek-a-boo.**

For reasons understood perhaps only by experts in early childhood development, audiences are very amused when objects or people appear, disappear, and then reappear on stage. This is especially effective in doorways and windows.

91. **The best judge of humor is the audience.**
The audience will find jokes and meaning you never knew were there.

Take comfort in knowing that in professional productions, valuable discoveries frequently take place during previews, when test audiences tell a cast (and the director) some of what's really going on in the play.

There is no shame in discovering that the audience sees things you do not. Pay close attention to their collective wisdom.

92. **Proper audience focus is key to an effective joke.**
A genuinely funny line wasn't laughed at. Why? Someone may have moved, coughed, or otherwise stolen audience attention at an inopportune moment.

93. **If a joke's not working, try reversing positions.**
Depending on the theatre—and the actors—it is possible that the joke will be more effective when the audience is watching the receiver's face, not the speaker's.

94. **Good humor requires a bad disposition.**

Jay Leno once commented that a good comedian requires two assets: good jokes and a bad attitude. You
need both because good jokes will sometimes fall
flat. Blame it on the weather, the delivery, the time
of day. No matter—the performer will need something else to fall back on. Rude or quirky behaviour
works just fine.

IX

Elements of Staging

95. If it moves, the eye will follow.

To control the audience's gaze, put an object in motion. No eye can resist.

This is a critical tenet of stage direction since the audience is free to look wherever they like.

If more than one object is in motion at the same time, the eye will track to whichever object was most recently set in motion or was most newly revealed *by* the motion. When motion is combined with sound, however, the eye will look in that direction regardless of whatever else might be happening.

A shift in light will also appear as movement to the eye and is among the director's most powerful tools for controlling the audience's focus.

96. Every object tells.

In a properly created on-stage world, nothing is extra

and nothing is missing. (Recall 13. Realize that the end is in the beginning.)

To paraphrase Chekhov, "Never hang a musket over the fireplace in Act I unless someone gets shot in Act III." That is, do not create visual anticipation without exploiting it.

Playwright Romulus Linney stated this same idea more strongly: "Everything on the set should be used up, burned up, blown up, destroyed, or otherwise completely chemically altered over the course of the story or else it didn't belong there to begin with."

97. Love triangles.

Two actors on stage establish a single visual relationship. Add just one more actor and you have up to seven relationships: one relationship between any two of the individuals (that's three relationships), one for each of the possible pairings of two individuals in opposition to the third (that's three more), plus the unique relationship that exists between all three.

Look for threes. When you have a triangular situation—and therefore rich dramatic possibilities—make clear choices as to who is in opposition to whom and how alliances and allegiances shift moment by moment. (Recall 53. Every scene is a chase scene.)

98. **When few characters are on stage in a large space, keep them apart.**

Space between characters creates tension as well as greater possibilities for physical and psychological maneuvering.

When blocking, imagine an elastic band connects the characters. When they come together, the tension is gone, the chase is over. (Recall 54. The strength of the characters' wants equals the strength of the play.) Look for ways and reasons to separate them, to reestablish the tension, the chase, the very reason for watching.

99. **Imbalance adds interest.**

Bilateral symmetry can be boring. Unbroken lines can be boring. This is true for sets, furniture, and actor placement. Severity, balance, and formality have dramatic value in specific instances, but not generally.

In staging the play, value the diagonal, the visual interruption, the rough.

100. **Choose a facing angle.**

When an actor faces an audience straight on, each audience member will feel he or she is being addressed directly. A slightly angled address prevents this, if you want it prevented.

101. Stand up.
Seating an actor suggests a long, boring scene will follow. If you can find a credible excuse for the actors to stand, use it. (Lighting a cigarette or pouring a drink have often been used for this purpose, albeit now with heavy cliché baggage attached.)

102. Don't stand still.
If for some reason the actor must remain in place, there must be meaning and intention in the non-movement. The standing character must either be interested or repelled. She must desperately *want* to move, but cannot. Or she is immoveable, adamant, standing as if reaching the stars and sky. Or she is moved to stillness.

103. Sit down, if you're up to it.
Royalty sit in chairs, not on stairs, floors, or boxes. They always walk in straight lines, regardless of who is in their way. It is the reaction of *others* that defines royal status: nonroyalty get out of the way...*fast*. The alternative is certain and sudden death.

Note, too, that there are many forms of royalty to whom this reactive behaviour might apply. In his realm, for instance, Al Capone was royalty.

104. **An audience's interest in the action is only as high as the actors' interest in it.**
Keep an eye out for disinterested responses such as yawning or an actor's gazing upon anything other than what the audience should be looking at.

Watch extras in large groups, especially. They frequently steal vital focus by being negative listeners, hating everything they hear.

Here's the rule: Listener reactions that are positive and interested focus audience attention on the *speaker*. Listener reactions that are negative and disinterested steal attention away from the speaker and toward the *listener*.

105. **Listening is active.**
The audience should (usually) know how the characters feel about what they're hearing. Feelings are conveyed through the body: Yes, I agree with that (and so I will approach); no, I disagree somewhat with that (and so will retreat slightly); I'll shut-up here (and let my hesitation cause my opponent to

squirm); I'll threaten with an approach there...(Recall 54. The strength of the characters' wants equals the strength of the play, and 55. Ask: Is it nice or nasty? Big or little?)

106. Character reactions should be active and outward, not passive and inward.

ACTIVE: "Don't *do* that!

PASSIVE: "Oh, don't do *that!*"

107. Turn your back.

Strength and confidence in staging can be indicated by occasionally having an actor turn his or her back to the audience. This is not, however, a good choice for the first time we encounter a character, nor for long speeches.

108. Give your actors face time.

Basic but often forgotten: When choosing props and furniture, be mindful of upstaging the actors with, for example, tall candlesticks or a high table.

Hats, too, often obscure the face. If it is absolutely necessary to keep the hats on, it will be absolutely necessary to continually remind the actors to keep their hats and their heads up.

109. Style has its reasons.

Elements of style are best applied with intention, purpose, and meaning—not as ends in themselves.

A character in a Restoration drama, for instance, bows with open palms extended away from his body to demonstrate he has no weapons. Ironically, this may also indicate he still wants them, needs them, or has them hidden somewhere.

A woman desperately waving a perfumed handkerchief as she speaks does so to hide her atrocious breath.

Without intention, style is empty.

110. Consider if you're missing a costume moment.

Costume designer Patton Campbell once said every play should have at least one costume moment. I don't know if this is true and have only vague ideas about what it really means, but it can't hurt to look for one.

111. Respect the power of music.

Music has the ability, second perhaps only to scent, to bypass our emotional defenses. In a director's hands, therefore, music is a powerful tool for guiding the audience's emotional experience.

Don't throw this power away. Don't use music indiscriminately. Don't choose music that has only a strong personal connection for *you*. Ask instead how the music you select might guide someone else's feelings, someone *unlike* you.

Lyrics are especially dangerous in this regard because others might interpret them differently than you. Are they hearing the same lyrics as you? Are they even listening to the lyrics *at all*?

112. **Use sound to prompt the audience to imagine the unseen, off-stage world.**

Consider, for example, having characters occasionally say beginning lines off stage, *then* having them enter.

113. **Acting solutions are always better than technical solutions.**

Enough said.

114. **Beware the naked truth.**

Yes, nudity might bring in a crowd, but at what cost? Earnest nudity imposed by sincere directors is rarely the reliable conveyer of inner emotional nakedness and vulnerability they suppose it is.

More typically, when the skin makes its appearance, the audience is ripped from the world of the play along with the clothing. The audience is deposited in a prurient inner world far from the plot. Their eyes no longer watch the eyes, mouths, and hands of the performers, but are diverted, no, *riveted* to other body parts. The audience and the story often become lost to each other.

X

Last Tips

115. When a scene isn't clicking, the entrance was probably wrong.

Work on what happens before the scene begins.

116. Blocking problem?

Ask yourself, and the actor, what do the lines suggest the character is *doing*? What is she trying to accomplish?

Occupy your actors. They will not lose sincerity or become overly self-conscious when they feel useful and engaged.

117. When a scene is well acted, clearly understood, and boring...

...the actors are probably behaving as if they had all the time in the world. But they haven't; at any moment some other character could enter and destroy the chase, some outside event could thwart the chaser.

You as director must make sure that they are aware of this. ("She'll be here any minute!" "The train is leaving the station!") The knowledge that they have only a limited amount of time imparts an urgency that would hurl the scene forward at breakneck speed were it not for the other factors—the need to disguise a motive, the fear of being misunderstood—that slow the action down and create tension.

Get them to listen to a Toscanini recording of, say, Brahms' First Symphony. Marvel at the tension he creates, moving the music as fast as it can possibly go. Because of the resistance to its forward motion, the tempo ends up relatively slow, but it doesn't *feel* slow because the sense of wanting to move ahead is so strong and the oppositions—the inner voices, the grinding harmonies that threaten to drown the main melody—are so interesting.

Similarly, every scene in every play wants to move as fast as humanly possible. Again, this may involve passages of extreme slowness, but you'll never bore an audience as you will with something that slips along efficiently and easily against a mere token resistance.

118. **When a scene is well timed, well acted, clearly understood, and STILL boring…**

    …an element of pleasure is likely missing.

    In our lives we say and do things because they give us satisfaction. Eating, drinking, watching TV, crying, refusing to speak, breaking a favorite ornament—all are paths to pleasure, to make us feel better.

    It's the same on stage. Unless characters are seen to be satisfying some need by what they do and say, the performance will be correct but bloodless.

    Let's consider a great piece of acting on film: Edith Evans as Lady Bracknell. It is striking how greedy she appears, how she chews on her lines as if they were pieces of well-cooked steak. Even in the boniest, harshest piece of Strindberg, the characters are all striving toward satisfaction, pleasure, and it's your job as director to make sure that the actors convey this.

    Take as your watchword the character in Chekhov's *Ivanov* who does not say, "How bored I am," but "I'm *so* bored, I could beat my head against a wall!" An extreme remedy for an extreme condition.

119. **Listen for overzealous vocal entrances.**

    When actors enter with full voice or on a high note, they can't go anywhere as the scene progresses except to take it down. Scenes tend to be better when they build, so do voices. Unless the script clearly calls for something different, start low and then build.

120. **Listen for actors who drop the ends of lines.**

You know you're in trouble when it sounds like the last line of another play but you're only in the middle of Act I. This habit will quickly wear an audience down.

Since downward inflections are often triggered by commas and periods in the script, they are a reliable indicator that an actor is "seeing the page" rather than engaging in what's actually happening on stage. If you can't break the habit, tell the actor to imagine an ellipsis ("…") in place of the printed punctuation.

121. **An actor is lost in his role…**

…not playing correctly—too angry, too timid, etc. Don't analyze the part for him. Don't do it for him. Don't criticize. There's a perfectly effective and impartial way to do it. You can simply say, "He's not angry here. He's very secure in himself, very sure, very self-satisfied, very definite." In other words, the character is not the way he seems to be coming across now, but this other way. Positive direction, clarity, and simplicity have their uses.

122. **An actor dries completely on his lines in performance…**

    …draws a complete blank and freezes up. Do you whip him? Scream? Torture him? No. You don't feel as badly as he does. Offer encouragement: "It was good that it happened at a preview, not an opening." "Everyone comes close to such a moment at some time." "We're all just a hair's breadth away from it happening to us, fate just caught you." "We're all human." Consider using an offstage prompter if it becomes a chronic problem.

123. **If an actor abuses you publicly, stay calm.**

    It's always unpleasant, but nine times out of ten it arises from mild hysteria that will cool down if you don't try to confront it head-on. The tenth time you have a problem. Just hang on to one simple fact: You don't have to be humiliated unless you want to be. The cast will be on your side. If need be, break the rehearsal for ten minutes and see what happens.

124. **Don't lose your cool.**

    Expressing anger publicly may feel justified at times but it often just makes you look like a fool. The only time that getting visibly and audibly angry will help you is when you make the choice to display anger as a conscious tactic to motivate an individual who has not responded to logic, reason, kindness, charm, diplomacy, or bribery. (Recall 26. You perform most of the day.)

125. Watch for and value happy accidents.

Mistakes like a hat falling off or a missed entrance are sometimes extremely valuable. They are not simply mistakes, but bits of reality entering into the pretend situation of rehearsal or performance.

In the same vein, when someone (an assistant stage manager, for instance) fills in for an actor during rehearsals, the other actors' line recall or blocking may be disturbed slightly. This is a small price to pay for the jolt of freshness and insight it can provide. Pay close attention.

126. Got a great moment? Do it again.

Whenever a happy accident occurs, have the actors do it again with no intervening commentary. Creating a great moment is one thing, but much of its value to the play depends on honest repeatability.

127. Got a great moment? Keep it to yourself.

Don't celebrate a great moment too much. You'll

annoy the actors and may never get the moment back. (Recall 89. Actors must never aim for the laugh.)

128. **Some things are not and should not be repeatable.** If you have skilled actors at work, there will be some variations moment to moment and performance to performance that make it real and therefore subject to change. Expect and accept that. Do not attempt to simultaneously mandate the revelation of real life on stage *and* the repeatability of dictated, on-the-nose moments. They are often mutually exclusive.

Audiences come to the theatre because live performance—at its best—can make us feel more connected and alive, as if we are part of the important and real events occurring on stage *right now*. As in sports, it should feel as if anything could happen at any moment.

Such real and true moments can be a bit messy, unpredictable, wonderful, spontaneous, dangerous... and very difficult to repeat.

Rather than exerting your control over it all, dedicate yourself to keeping the life between actors alive. Do your part to combat that great, common misconception that acting is, at its heart, lying, controlled fakery, or deception. Don't micromanage.

Decide what you will allow to live and flourish without all your potentially damaging or inhibiting intervention. (Recall 27. It is not about you, and 61. Sincerely praise actors early and often.)

129. **Don't hold the audience captive during a long scene change.**

Give them a break. With any scene change longer than half a minute, bring the house lights up to half. It is better to have the audience rustling through the program than to have them wondering if something's wrong backstage. Of course, something might very well be wrong backstage—all the more reason to bring up the lights and let them read to distraction.

130. **How to handle critics...**

A. Calm your actors and give them perspective with this advice: "Ultimately, you are in a better position than anyone else to understand the value of your own experience, so decide in advance what your opinion of this work is. Then you can judge what is valuable and what is not in the forthcoming review."

That takes care of the intellect. The ego is another issue.

B. Rosemary Clooney's advice to her nephew, George Clooney: "You're never as good as they say you are when they say you're good, but you're never as bad as they say you are when they say you're bad."

C. Director Marshall Mason tells his casts not to read reviews. He is not as concerned, he says, about the effect of the negative critiques as he is the effusive ones; "She collapsed across the veranda like a lost piece of history" is pretty difficult to recreate night after night.

D. About critics, playwright David Ives cleverly remarked, "Ultimately one has to pity these poor souls who know every secret of writing, directing, designing, producing, and acting but are stuck in those miserable day jobs writing reviews. Will somebody help them, please?"

Epilogue

Your first, second, and third duty is to the author. After that come the actor, the audience, the producer, or anyone else.

The author tells everyone what to do, but the instructions are in code. Being a director means cracking that code, interpreting, not to demonstrate how clever you are, but to get out of the way, to let the actors show the play in clear to the audience. Your job is to prevent any changes in the script unless you are honestly convinced by repeated trial that change is essential. You must come up with no "concept" of the play that means omitting passages which don't fit, altering an emphasis for the sake of novelty, or twisting the writer's overt intention in order to bring out some hypothetical Inner Meaning.

In other words, be honest.

The current fondness for updating texts—Shakespeare, the Greeks—is basically a form of snobbery: "How amusing! They're quite like us!" As if there were anything to be said for dragging Medea or Hamlet into our appalling time. Contrariwise, if the plays are well presented in their own period, we have the far more fascinating and educative experience of time travel, going back across the centuries and finding out how like them *we* are.

Keep in mind that what is new is not necessarily good because it is new. What is old, however, is worthy of our respect, attention, and study because it *is* old, because it has lasted.

APPENDIX I

The What Game

Most actors feel deep down that they have better things to do than make every single word mean something; after all, we speak the same language, don't we? And so long as you can gather from "O what a rogue and peasant slave am I" that Hamlet is deeply upset about something, the audience will pick up enough of the text to follow what's going on…and that leaves room for lots of lovely acting…

DIRECTOR: Would you please recite "Mary Had A Little Lamb?"

ACTOR: "Mary had a little lamb / Its fleece was white as snow / And everywhere that Mary went / The lamb was sure to go."

DIRECTOR: Once again, please. And this time I'll stop you when I'm not sure I understand.

ACTOR: "Mary had…"

DIRECTOR: Who had?

ACTOR: MARY. "MARY had a little lamb…"

DIRECTOR: She still has it?

ACTOR: Yes.

DIRECTOR: So it's, "Mary HAS a little lamb?"

ACTOR: No. "Mary HAD a little…"

DIRECTOR: Who had?

ACTOR: "MARY HAD a little lamb…"

DIRECTOR: A medium lamb?

ACTOR: "A LITTLE lamb…"

Appendix 1: The What Game

DIRECTOR: A little what?

ACTOR: "A LITTLE LAMB…"

DIRECTOR: From the beginning, please.

ACTOR: "MARY HAD a LITTLE LAMB / Its fleece
was white…"

DIRECTOR: Fleece is dull, soggy?

ACTOR: No, springy.

DIRECTOR: All again, please.

ACTOR: "MARY has a LITTLE LAMB…"

DIRECTOR: Has it now?

ACTOR: "MARY HAD a LITTLE LAMB / Its FLEECE
was white…"

DIRECTOR: Fairly clean?

ACTOR: "WHITE as SNOW…"

And so on.

The effect of *The What Game* is like the cleaning of an old picture: it shows what treasures lie concealed.

The actors detest it to begin with. "I suppose you want me to punch every word?"

"Well, it's better than mumbling half of them."

Quickly, though, they see the value of it. Pace and common sense will take care of overemphasis.

The game has the added advantage that actors can also play it (silently or openly) with each other.

APPENDIX II

Friends & Enemies

The Invisible Audience

We all carry with us an invisible audience that from time to time emerges and joins in our action. Its members purr with pleasure when we make an ingeniously biting remark. They laugh silently at our well-turned witticism. They are indignant on our behalf when we speak out against some injustice.

People in plays often act to this audience, sometimes almost imperceptibly (Trigorin in *Three Sisters*), sometimes blatantly (Malvolio is constantly interrupted by applause from his invisible admirers—they never disagree with him, any more than ours do with us). King Lear carries with him an entourage that no daughter can dismiss, egging him on to ever more apocalyptic behaviours.

It may sound far-fetched, but anyone who saw Margaret Thatcher in her later days as Prime Minister would have noticed her follow up some flashing put-down with a look all about her so satisfied, so responsive, that one could almost hear the imaginary cries of: "Well done, Maggie!" "That's the spirit, Maggie!" "You show 'em, Maggie!"

Subjects and Objects

Accept the premise that some people are predominantly *Subjects* (as in the subject of a sentence, *not* in the royal sense of monarch and subject). Subjects are in command, they make the rules, they *act*. The verb is theirs. Above all, they are the ones who *look*. Others are *Objects*; they are aware of *being looked at*, of being acted upon, of being made to conform to another's will. (We all, of course, change roles from time to time, Subject or Object, depending whether we are talking to the paperboy or our ex-headmaster.)

Often in plays the underlying dynamic consists of A trying to force B into the role of Object. He will keep him waiting before speaking; when he does speak, it will be from an angle that compels B to shift in order to see him. He will chase B by moving away while talking, so that B has to follow in order to hear what is being said. In particular, A tries to make B feel unable and consequently ashamed and consequently likely to do whatever A wants. For A is never ashamed; he can feel guilty, but that can be suppressed, unlike shame. The classic example is Iago turning Othello from Subject (military commander, successful lover) into Object (horribly aware that everyone is looking at him, laughing at him). Once Othello bases his behaviour on "What People Will Think," he is no longer his own master; Iago can destroy him piecemeal.

Simplicity, Variety, and Clarity

Simplicity

John Gielgud had one word of advice for young actors: "Relax."

Here's the rule: The audience will generally believe whatever they are told to believe by the script until they are given a reason not to believe it.

The term *overacting* has become synonymous with bad acting because so much ineffective performance is due to an actor doing too much, demonstrating and explaining too much to an audience. In doing so, the actor creates too many opportunities to do something that is not entirely accurate, something that reveals the falsity of the pretend situation.

Doing too much also betrays an untrustworthy overabundance of effort. It makes people suspicious:

"What's he compensating for?" "What's she hiding?" (And when the other characters don't pick up on this false behaviour—because it's not in the script to do so—the audience can be excused for thinking everyone up there is an idiot.) Better for the actor to create fewer opportunities for the audience to disbelieve.

So tell your actors to relax, keep it simple, and dare to do less. Advise them to watch the great actors and notice how little they do—how little they *push*—and then notice the spare, important actions they *do* choose. (See 66. Keep actors on their task.) A good actor can be simple and consistent *and* interesting all at the same time. Cultivate these qualities in your actors. (See 128. Some things are not and should not be repeatable.)

Variety
On the other hand, variety can be an important component of storytelling, as we know from the contrasting expressions and wide range of gestures we use in telling stories to children.

Most of us, for example, speak too flatly. An actor must be able to convey meaning to an audience, which is accomplished through variety in speed, volume, and pitch as well as contrast in action, movement, and pacing.

To help exercise these qualities, have the actors play *The What Game* (appendix 1). They hate it but there is no substitute.

There *are* limits to variety, however. Actors should avoid, for instance, playing doubles such as "Fie! fie!" or "Come, come" as separate thoughts. They're just a single impulse—no variety needed.

Clarity

So which is it, simplicity or variety? The test here is for clarity. If, in your particular circumstances, variety clarifies, adds meaning, and is likely to keep the audience interested, pursue it. If it obfuscates, complicates, or distracts, simplicity is the path.

Too many audiences blame themselves for not following a story when their negative experiences may in fact be the result of directing that undervalues clarity and demonstrates an ethos of "Good Art Is What You Cannot Understand."

This misguided approach grows from a romantic notion that great ideas and those who think them are valued by the degree to which they're *misunderstood*. There are historical precedents for the suffering genius, but deliberately inducing confusion for self-pro-motional purposes is hardly the route to winning over an audience. Confused audiences may be lost forever, thinking theatre and art in general are not for them.

This is a crime.

APPENDIX IV

Meaning It

There is only one intensive in English: the word "fuck" (or "fucking").

Listen to the actor declaiming:

> *O! What a rogue and peasant slave am I!*

Note how he strains to make the derogatory language sound real, as if he really means it. Get him to put in a few "fuckings:"

> *O! What a fucking rogue and peasant*
> *fucking slave am I!*

Hear how it immediately hardens and sharpens the images, makes them more like real anger and real self-disgust rather than disguised self-pity. Not just impressive but meant.

Should you keep these word substitutions in performance?

No.

. . .

There is another dimension to all this. All soliloquies, whether delivered to the (paying) audience or kept within the confines of the stage, are all really conversations beneath their surface.

There is the "you" voice—nagging, blaming, accusing, familiar from a thousand interior arguments:

> YOU: You've got to get out of bed.

In opposition there is always the "I" voice—self-justifying, resentful:

> I: I need just a few minutes more.

> YOU: You always say that. You're going to be late again.

> I: That's not fair. I'm never late.

Appendix IV: Meaning It

YOU: Don't make me laugh. And you haven't even got a clean shirt...

...and so on.

To make this exchange clear, get the actor to split the two voices. Actually change the pronouns temporarily and then listen to the difference, especially with a few "fuckings" thrown in:

YOU: ~~Yet I~~ *But you* / a dull and muddy-mettled rascal, peak, / Like a *fucking* John-a-dreams, unpregnant of ~~my~~ *your* cause, / And can say ~~nothing~~ *fuck-all*...

I: Who calls me villain? Breaks my pate across...?

YOU: 'Swounds, ~~I should~~ *you would fucking* take it, for it cannot be / But ~~I am~~ *you are* pigeon-livered and lack gall / To make oppression bitter...

Hamlet Act II, Scene 2

If spoken with real conviction, the lines will emerge with a true note of rage and contempt turned inward against the speaker.

APPENDIX V

Recommended Reading

A ny serious student of directing should read, well, everything: dictionaries, literature, treatises, newspapers, cereal boxes... Get in the habit of mining the world for inspiration. Of course, don't miss the standard texts, including Aristotle's *Poetics*; Stanislavski's trilogy, *An Actor Prepares*, *Building a Character*, and *Creating a Role* (note the clever "A, B, C" of the title sequence); and Richard Boleslavski's *Acting: The First Six Lessons.*

. . .

Here are some additional recommendations:

A Sense of Direction: Some Observations on the Art of Directing by William Ball
ISBN: 0-89676-082-0

Drama Book Publishers, New York, 1984
> Lessons from a lifetime of directing. Authoritative and thoughtful, accessible and sensible.

Elia Kazan: A Life by Elia Kazan
ISBN: 0-385-26103-9
Anchor Books, Doubleday, New York, 1989
> The inside story of a great director's life and career. Filled with honest, valuable observations. Unsanitized for your inspection.

On Directing by Harold Clurman
ISBN: 0-02-013350-2
Collier Books, New York, 1972
> One of the most respected American directors (and Kazan's mentor) expounds on the craft and his practice of it. Includes helpful and articulate discussions of what is variously known as a play's "spine," "through-action," "super problem," or "main action"—an understanding of which is central to any director's authority and responsibility.

Appendix v: Recommended Reading

Brewer's Dictionary of Phrase and Fable, 16th edition by
Ebenezer Cobham Brewer, Adrian Room, and Terry
Pratchett
ISBN: 0-06019-653-X
HarperCollins, New York, 2000
> A priceless reference tool. Mythological, reli-
> gious, and literary references explained.

Envisioning Information by Edward R. Tufte
ISBN: 0-9613921-1-8
Graphics Press, Cheshire, Connecticut, 1990

Visual Explanations by Edward R. Tufte
ISBN: 0-9613921-2-6
Graphics Press, Cheshire, Connecticut, 1997
> The director's craft is largely visual. These
> bibles of visual thinking, written by one of the
> world's leading information designers, are not
> just about effective visual communication but
> are also outstanding exemplars of it.

Picture This: How Pictures Work by Molly Bang
ISBN 1-58717-030-2
SeaStar Books, New York, 1991, 2000

An artist's entertaining and enlightening ex-
ploration of how shapes, colors, and pictures
tell. Indispensable information for any director.

Mastering the Techniques of Teaching, 2nd edition by
Joseph Lowman
ISBN: 0-7879-5568-X
Jossey-Bass, San Francisco, 1995
All good directors are, in large part, teachers.
And all good teachers know the importance of
dramatization. This excellent book under-
stands the link, and more.

A Pattern Language by Christopher Alexander, Sara
Ishikawa, Murray Silverstein, *et al.*
ISBN: 0-19-501919-9
Oxford University Press, New York, 1977
Not applicable to directing *per se*, but a must-
read for anyone interested in the codification
of objective standards within what are nor-
mally considered subjective realms—in this
case, the built world of architectural design.
One of the great books of the last century.

Appendix v: Recommended Reading

Stage Directors Handbook, 2nd edition, prepared by Stage Directors and Choreographers Foundation, edited by John P. Bruggen and Joe Miloscia.
ISBN 1-55936-150-6
Theatre Communications Group, New York, 2003
> A comprehensive resource for anyone interested in a directing career.
> See also *www.sdcfoundation.org*

Acknowledgments

I have had the great pleasure and good fortune to learn with many wonderful teachers. Frank Hauser stands out not only as my coauthor but also as my mentor. It is to him, directly or indirectly, that I owe the majority of the teachings contained here. Thank you, Frank, for your trust, kindness, wisdom, humility, and generosity.

Other teachers who made a significant contribution to my understanding of theatrecraft—and whom I remember gratefully—include: Robin Wagner, Howard Stein, Atlee Sproul, Norman R. Shapiro, Mark Ramont, Austin Quigley, Steven Philips, Edward Petherbridge, Marshall Mason, Jeff Martin, David Mamet, Ted Lorenz, Romulus Linney, Jacques Levy, Alex Kinney, Peter Jefferies, Paul Hart, Imero Fiorentino, Michael Feingold, Ron Eyre, Patton Campbell, Tanya Berezin, and Norman Ayrton.

Special acknowledgment is due to those who demonstrated extraordinary generosity in lending their professional expertise to the creation of this book. My sincere gratitude to:

Evan Butts for legal counsel; Steven Rivellino, Jane Slotin, Joe Witt, and Jeff Martin for creative guidance; Julia Reich for the jacket design; Robin Nelson, Jeffrey Korn, Matthew and Lee Kane, Gail Goodman, William Ganis, Karen Finkel, and Joan Albert for their creative contributions; Connie Paul for her research support; Jerry Zaks, Robin Wagner, Sir Ian McKellen, Mark Lamos, Rosemary Harris, Rupert Graves, Sir Richard Eyre, Dame Judi Dench, Mark Capri, and Edward Albee for their kind endorsements; Brian and Nina Taylor and Michael Morris of Pneuma Books for their production review and internal design; and Rupert and Susie Graves, Eric Hauser, Laurence Harbottle, Ayalah Haas, Fabrizio Almeida, Caroline Sands, Clayton Philips, Toby Robertson, and Ellen Novack for their various efforts on behalf of the book.

For reviewing the manuscript and contributing valuable suggestions, sincere thanks to Joe Witt, Joanna Smith, Jane Slotin, Nan Satter, Steven Rivellino, Jeff Martin, Jeffrey Korn, Rebecca Friedman, Jane Cummins, and Tony Castrigno.

Acknowledgments

I offer additional acknowledgment for support and inspiration to: Dr. Joel Warshowsky, Julie Robbins, Joel Nissan, Phyllis Blackman, and Alisa Adler. Also, David Swenson, Tom Strodel, Shanda Stiles, Sarah Stiles, Dr. David and Aline Smolanoff, Jane Scimeca, Dr. Kurt Schulz, Gary and Evelyn Reich, Matthew and Marla Reich, Jordana Reich, Ethan Reich, Dan Plice, Garda Parker, Dr. Gary Ostrow, John Oppenhimer, Lauren Newman, Victoria McGinnis, Wendy Miller, Eileen and Brandy McCann, Blaine Lucas, Debbie Landau, Alan and Ronit Karben, Bradley and Lisa Hurley, Shellee Hendriks, Dr. R. Glenn Hessel, Mike Green, Greg and Val Goetchius, Scott and Maureen Fichten, Patrick Edwards, Dr. Jordan Dimitrakov, Michelle and Alan Cutler, Nicole Barnett, and David Ball and Farah Brelvi.

Index

Index

Index

Index

personality
    actor communication,
        46
    casting, 17–18
Petherbridge, Edward, 53
playwright
    centrality of, 79–80
    intention notes, 24
pleading gestures, tells, 36
pleasure, problem tips, 71
plot, characters and, 35
posture, staging elements,
    62, 64
practicalities, first read-
    through, 23
praise, actor communica-
    tion, 40, 47
preparation, director's
    role, 12
previews, humor, 55
problems
    rehearsal rules, 30
    tips on, 69–77
professional relationships
    casting, 19–20

director's role, 12–13
professionalism
    casting, 17–19
    director's role, 9
props. *see* objects

Q

questioning
    actor communication,
        45
    first read-through, 24

R

rehearsal rules, 27–31, 39.
    see also actors
relationships (profession-
    al). *see* professional
    relationships
repeatability, problem
    tips, 74–75
resistance
    actor communication,
        42–43
    strength, 34–35
resolution, script and, 5–6

Index

For quantity purchases or special needs, contact:

Pathway Book Service
4 White Brook Road
Gilsum, NH 03448
Toll free: 1-800-345-6665
Email to: pbs@pathwaybook.com

Notes on Directing is also available through Ingram,
Baker & Taylor, and other wholesalers.

Reader opinion and feedback are welcome. Please
contact the publisher via *www.notesondirecting.com*

The body of this book is set in *Spectrum*, which is based on the design by Jan van Krimpen in 1943 for the Spectrum Publishing House. Spectrum was completed and released by the Monotype Corporation in 1955, although the Bible project it was originally commissioned for was never completed. Spectrum is known for its readability; its roots reach directly to Venetian typefaces of the 15th century. Its varied-weight curves and angular serifs evoke the calligraphic pen strokes of its forebearers.

Mrs. Eaves, used on the cover and for chapter titles in the interior, was designed by Zuzana Licko for Emigré in 1996 as a reprise of the Transitional typeface *Baskerville*, crafted in 1757. The name, Mrs. Eaves, comes from John Baskerville's maid, Sarah Eaves, who became his wife after the death of her first husband. Like Spectrum, Baskerville was originally designed for use in a Bible. The beauty and versatility of Mrs. Eaves allow for its use as both a display and a body typeface.

Cover design by Julia Reich

Interior design by Pneuma Books, LLC.
www.pneumabooks.com

Printed in the United States by Thomson-Shore, Inc.